MW00612068

Cornelius Vanderbilt
The Commodore

Cornelius Vanderbilt
The Commodore

Insight and Analysis Into the Life and Success of America's First Tycoon

J.R. MacGregor

Cornelius Vanderbilt – The Commodore

Published by CAC Publishing LLC

ISBN 978-1-950010-35-6 paperback

ISBN 978-1-950010-34-9 eBook

Table of Contents

Introduction..7
Chapter 1 America at the end of the 18th Century
(politics, economics, and social)...............................16
Chapter 2 New York Trade and Industry.................27
Chapter 3 The Vanderbilts Before the 19th Century30
Chapter 4 Cornelius 42
Chapter 5 Enterprise and Negotiation......................49
Chapter 6 1812...60
Chapter 7 Converging Heritage 67
Chapter 8 Opportunist...77
Chapter 9 Steamers and Boilers...............................86
Chapter 10 Steamboat Captain.................................93
Chapter 11 Being One's Own Man........................102
Chapter 12 What Goes Around..............................109
Chapter 13 The Advent of Rail..............................122
Chapter 14 Better Quarters 133
Conclusion 140

Introduction

Not many people would like the life that Cornelius Vanderbilt I lived. To many, his ways may seem uncouth and his methods beyond the pale. Before judging, however, it is best to remember that this was the Wild West of the 1800s. Placing twenty-first century ideals on nineteenth century life is not exactly being fair.

The Commodore himself probably wouldn't care about how one felt about him. Many people insulted him to his face, but it never bothered him at all. He was too busy to be offended.

What one should know about America in general and New York in particular, where he grew up, is that they were very different places then compared with where we are now. The differences in lifestyle, thinking, the environment, law, and politics were different in absolute terms. The only thing that remains similar is that the composition of New York then and now has always been ethnically, culturally, and religiously diverse.

What worked then to make it big still works today. If you look closely and choose to look beyond the crass words and tawdry actions, what you end up seeing is a boy who grew up with a very specific focus in life. He could not see anything else. All he wanted to do was take advantage of every possible situation and fight hard to stake his claim.

Thousands of immigrants were coming here and heading out to the territories to stake their claim in a new land, but Vanderbilt staked his claim right where he was born. He had elevated the game without a shred of education much less an education in some fancy academic setting.

By climbing and altering the way businesses were run, he set up the infrastructure for the next generation of industrialists to build on top of it. When the United States was in its early stages, Vanderbilt saw the importance of sea travel. He saw the importance of having a canal run through the isthmus in Central America long before it became a national security imperative to dredge the Panama Canal. It was Vanderbilt who spoke to the leaders of Nicaragua and obtained a lease for the land that extended from the Pacific to the Atlantic, a distance of 150 miles.

It was his idea to consolidate the fragmented railroads that came into New York, and it was his idea to build Grand Central Station, which still stands in New York City today. All this and more Vanderbilt did in a way that was focused and without distraction on the niceties of everyday living. He did whatever he wanted without caring for anyone's impressions or comments.

His character is worthy of study for those who wish to take the world stage by storm. The first lesson you will learn is that he never took anyone seriously—not in a hilarious and joking sort of way—but he never allowed anyone's ideas to influence his own mind and thinking. No one except perhaps his mother could influence him once he made up his mind.

It may be easy to fall into the trap of thinking that would be the best way to never learn, but in

Vanderbilt's case, it didn't turn out that way. He actually listened intently but never told anyone that he actually did. He was in search of ideas and thoughts, but it had to be something that he thought of—the point being that he was too strong to blindly follow another's ideas, thoughts, and advice.

He was also not the kind of person to give his money to charity. The only person he gave his wealth to was his favorite son. Everyone else didn't get much by comparison. He didn't believe in philanthropy or inheritance. What he believed in was vision and hard work. As clichéd as that sounds, Vanderbilt embodied it.

Of all the robber barons and titans who lived, Vanderbilt was probably the crassest. Some biographers have called him vulgar, and others have pointed to his lechery, but this book will not critique a man who who died almost 150 years ago. That is not the purpose of this book, and neither should it be for any biography. Biographies are intended to instruct us from beyond the grave as to a path that should be considered. It is not up to us to label a man or pass judgment on him based on our own moral and ethical constructs.

One specific and interesting aspect of Vanderbilt is that he had no interest in being someone that he says he is not. In other words, he didn't pretend to be one thing and then act differently. What you saw is what you got. That takes strength.

Take philanthropy, for instance. He never gave a cent to any cause. In fact, the bulk of his will passed to only one of his sons. He didn't give for the sake of giving or to alter public opinion. In Rockefeller's case, it was different. He went to great lengths to polish his legacy by recording videos and giving to charity amidst fanfare and publicity. He was a pioneer in modern-day public relations.

For Vanderbilt, there was no such thing as a public relations campaign. He was who he was. He had no intention of being portrayed as anything or anyone else. He didn't need to be someone he wasn't, and he didn't need his own persona to be advertised. He was not a hypocrite or a charlatan.

On his commercial side, he was a cutthroat competitor. He was a visionary but also an imbecile. He couldn't read well and wrote phonetically. He had no use for grammar, punctuation, or an extensive vocabulary. On his private side, he was lascivious. He didn't have a sliver of magnaminity in his body, but most of all he never tried to convince anyone that he wasn't any of these things. He stood proud of himself, and if you want to learn from him, you have to take him as you find him.

Vanderbilt knew that his fortunes did not come from whether he was virtuous or upstanding. It didn't come from how much philanthropy he engaged in or how well he treated his wife. It came from how much he could carry, how reliable his delivery was, and how much it cost. As long as he handled that aspect of it, it didn't matter what he did or didn't do in his private life.

He was pragmatic and found tremendous freedom in that. Even his ability to fight was not wasted on bar fights and brawls. He fought hard when he needed to, but as soon as the fight was over, he'd move on without any malice other than a note to remember the person he had just brawled with. It was his cargo and his customers that he wanted to satisfy. They didn't need to know anything about him except that they could trust that he was reliable and would deliver their goods safely.

What was particularly distinctive about Vanderbilt as he built his reputation in and around the harbor and then up and down the Hudson River, and then all the way down the coast, was that he always delivered what he promised. The peace of mind that he gave his customers was worth every penny they paid him. His reputation preceded him in that way. People sought him out and tried to get the best bargain, but when they only got the bargain that he dictated, they knew that was exactly what they would get.

Vanderbilt was the consummate opportunist. He didn't tie himself down to a rigid business plan or fix his schedule and activity. Other boat captains would just sail their periaugers, sloops, or schooners, specializing in one thing or another. If a boatman specialized in ferrying passengers from Port Richmond to Manhattan, then that is what he did day in, day out, almost all his life, but Vanderbilt was an opportunist who took on any load at any time as long as he was paid, and then he promptly and consistently delivered. This tied in with his desire to keep his vessels and later in life his trains full.

In his lifetime, he was one of very few people who were involved in a landmark Supreme Court case. The case would turn out to be the bedrock principle that dictated that the power to regulate interstate commerce was reserved to the federal government, and that states could no make law or enforce laws that were counter to federal law.

He built a solid base of steamships that grew from one to the next. He started sailing a 25-ton boat and finally built a 500-ton vessel that sailed down to Central America. The time that most men spend pondering and worrying about things that didn't matter Vanderbilt spent building his business.

Chapter 1 America at the end of the 18th Century (politics, economics, and social)

America had just declared its independence, but the battles Washington waged with Britain still raged on. We were formally declared as a country, but there still wasn't any leadership at the federal level. Washington was still leading armies in dozens of battles, from the Battle of Long Island in August 1776 to the Siege of Yorktown in October 1781.

From the time the dust settled after Yorktown, it took another six odd years for the Constitution to be written and another ten months for the states to ratify it. Until that point, the American government was given force by the Articles of Confederation.

Drafting of the Articles of Confederation started as soon as the Declaration of Independence was announced. It was submitted in a dozen days after the Declaration, but it took the Continental Congress more than a year to debate it and rewrite parts of it. At the heart of the problem that caused the delay was the issue of the powers that would be held by the national government.

Even before the Constitution was drafted, debated, and ratified, there was already a deep divide in the philosophy and principles of governing that preferred distributed governing rather than a centralized government. Based on their experience with Britain, no one wanted to cede their freedom to a concentrated center of power.

Once the Articles of Confederation had finally been ratified, it had departed somewhat from the original version drafted by John Dickerson. A compromise to leave some powers with the states and elevate some powers to the central government was reached. In its final format, the Articles of Confederation defined what the central government would be responsible for and that the rest would fall on the states to govern.

You can see that from the very beginning there was a split in the overall plan. Even with America born, the key issue was over who controlled what. Those who saw the value of collaborative unity saw the prosperity that could be achieved. Those who opposed a central power were still reeling from the effects of colonization and the power of London and the Crown over their lives. Both had a valid point to make.

Furthermore, under the Articles, the central government consisted of only a unicameral house (as opposed to the bicameral legislature we have now). There were no senators, just members of the House of Representatives who were chosen by the state's legislature. Regardless of land size or population, each state had only one vote in the House to ensure that the smaller states would not be ridden roughshod by the larger states. There was no provision for a president or an executive branch in any form, and there was no Supreme Court.

What's important to remember here is that there were two camps with a differing opinion. One wanted sovereignty over their own state, while the other wanted a centralized government so that they could bring about collective strength. That debate continues more than 250 years later in much of what we do and enact today.

The Constitution as we know it today didn't come about until 1787. It was in this Constitution that the Legislative, Executive, and Judicial branches of government were set up in Articles 1, 2, and 3 respectively. At the time of drafting the Constitution, there was yet another difference in opinion between those who saw the importance of unifying and those who were afraid of creating a new tyranny.

It wasn't until 1788 that General George Washington and sixty-five members of the House were elected. The Senate hadn't been set up yet and were originally chosen by the state legislatures unlike today's popular election in each state. It was only after the individual states had ratified the Constitution that two of each state's senators were chosen by their state's legislators and took their seat.

Once Congress was seated in April 1789, they passed the Judiciary Act pursuant to the requirement of Article 3 of the Constitution. This gave rise to the Supreme Court, which consisted of six justices at that time.

During the first few years following the Declaration of Independence, there weren't any political parties—no Republican or Democratic parties, no conservative or liberal groups—just newly minted Americans. The Founding Fathers were not inclined to adopt a party structure that had evolved elsewhere.

Early statesmen, such as Alexander Hamilton, Thomas Jefferson, and many others, did not initially believe in the need for political parties because they felt that they eroded the democratic process, put people and policies in silos, and brought unnecessary friction to a system that would work better when operated without friction.

Political parties only arose later because they were seen as the only tool available to organize the two sides of the divide. It is one of the reasons why the U.S. political system has been a two-party system. Before the parties got sidetracked by moral issues of liberalism and conservatism, they were arguing about where the power rested—with the states or the federal government.

The first party was formed in 1786 before the first election in 1788. The candidates, however, did not run on a specific party platform. When the party was finally organized, it was called the Federalist Party. As the name suggests, it believed in strong central governance and the need for the federal government to regulate, promote, control, and protect the states. They were primarily supported by bankers, businessmen, and the elite.

As soon as the Federalists came about to advocate the power of the federal government, the anti-Federalists were born to counter them. They were called the Democratic-Republicans, who were founded by Thomas Jefferson and James Madison. The debate over the adoption of the Constitution was vigorous. It was a time when the masses were consumed by politics and such people as Thomas Paine, who advocated the power of a strong federal government, wrote his pamphlet, *Common Sense*. It sold more than

150,000 copies, and James Madison wrote articles in the local newspaper that came to be known as the Federalist Papers.

In the end, the Constitution as it stood then could not be agreed upon between the Federalists and the anti-Federalists. The solution was to add ten additional amendments, which came to be known as the Bill of Rights. With that, the Constitution was ratified, elections were held, and the federal government started to take shape.

The adoption of the Constitution was a unique event and served, among other things, as the root of industrialization of the United States through the nineteenth century. That, in turn, formed the foundation for the success that the country enjoys today as the undisputed hegemony in today's geopolitical climate.

Before the Constitution was ratified and the subsequent industrialization, America was exclusively an agrarian society. Historians have zeroed in on the decade that saw the genesis of industrialization in America. Regardless of when other countries, namely Britain and France, underwent their industrial revolution, America's is deemed to have begun in 1790.

The 1790s, which can be seen as the decade in which a Constitutional America began, coincided with the introduction of industrial opportunities in addition to agrarian that had been the basis of the economy to this point. This went on until the 1860s when Abraham Lincoln was elected, the Confederate states seceded, and the Civil War ensued.

That period from 1790 to 1860 was critical in the development and foundation of America. On one side, immigrants were pouring in through numerous ports of entry, specifically New York. On the other side, resources from American agrarian efforts were being exported to the Old World. More than other ports in the North and South, New York bore the brunt of the heavy traffic. It also became the center for banking because farmers would receive and deposit money for their products and keep it in their banks in New York.

This made New York and the surrounding boroughs focused on banking, government (for a short period), shipping, insurance, and travel. As the city's population increased, the neighboring burroughs experiencd an increase in sea ferrying. There was no bridge yet to speak of—construction of the first major bridge, the New York Brooklyn Bridge (we know it today as the iconic Brooklyn Bridge), only started in 1869.

The only way goods and people traversed the waterways between the islands of the New York City area was by small ferries. The surrounding area of New York City, not just Manhattan but also the waterways between the various land masses, was one of the busiest places in the country at the time. It was crowded with all sizes of boats coming and going and little ferries shuttling between them.

The issue of federalism versus states' rights was a battle from the first time the idea of forming a union emerged. In today's context, this battle can sometimes be lost because we have now been one nation seemingly forever, but it was not always so. Even the Declaration of Independence was a marriage of convenience to place a united front against the British. It was partially thought of as a means to an end, but then the Federalist argument gained traction because there was so much more to gain. State versus federal control still remains a wide-ranging issue. One such issue involved commerce within the states. The Supreme Court battle that settled interstate commerce involved shipping, and by extension, Vanderbilt himself.

At the end of the eighteenth century, America was getting ready for the likes of the robber barons that were about to alter the way the world worked and civilizations operated. Andrew Carnegie, John D. Rockefeller, Henry Ford, and JP Morgan were men of extreme accomplishment that were yet to arrive on the scene and make a big difference in the way the story of America unfolded. Before them, however, was another man—Cornelius Vanderbilt I.

Chapter 2 New York Trade and Industry

Even though the U.S. capital had been moved to its new location, New York continued to prosper as the heart at the center of life. There were shipping agents, hotels, trading houses, and other activity that supported its core business of commerce and finance.

New York City is a city like no other. It is not a city that is all in one place or bisected by a river that runs through it. In New York, various boroughs exist on different land masses. The Bronx and Manhattan occupy one island, Queens and Brooklyn sit on another, and Staten Island, to the south, exists on its own. Across the bay was New Jersey, and none of this was connected by any tunnel or bridge that would transport people and cargo between the islands.

At the start of the nineteenth century, three businesses dominated the New York landscape.

The first and most important was the cotton industry, which featured cotton farmers who sent their cotton to New York to be loaded on ships bound for Britain. They were paid by buyers by way of New York banks.

Another product that was brought to New York was tobacco, which was then shipped to Europe. Tobacco farmers also deposited their proceeds from these activities with New York banks.

Besides these products were textiles, feed, corn and grain, and others.

Immigration was also increasing and considered a great resource for the country. It was also the inflow of new money and capital as well as new customers for everything from hotels to travel.

New York grew exponentially in the early part of the nineteenth century. As for Vanderbilt's success, aside from his own actions, his environment must be considered. It was a booming time for America in general and especially so for the development of New York Harbor and the city itself.

New York's dominance in the world of finance is entirely the result of the events that happened there at that time—from trading and shipping to banking and the railroad industry that flourished here to support the farmers who came from the inland states to export their produce as well as the imports that came from Europe—all converged on this small area.

From the day of his great-great-grandfather's arrival to the day he first piloted his own vessel in these waters, Vanderbilt's life is the story of New York itself. Vanderbilt was tough as nails, which was the only way to survive at the time.

As he grew, so did New York, and as New York flourished, so did he.

Chapter 3 The Vanderbilts Before the 19th Century

Holland was a powerful country in the seventeenth century. It controlled large amounts of trade and shipping routes in tropical South America and Asia. Holland was also the first to make a claim for land in New York, which was named New Amsterdam before the British renamed it New York in 1664.

When Jan Aertsen Van der Bilt left the Dutch town of Bilt, which was just a few miles from Utrecht, he did so as an indentured servant. In the seventeenth century, between half and two-thirds of the immigrants who came to work in North American colonies were indentured servants.

The typical agreement that existed in the 1600s between an indentured servant and his master is that in return for his work and expatriation to a new land he would receive full travel, board, and lodging and would remain the servant of the master for a set number of years—anywhere between three and five years or more. At the end of that period, he was paid a certain consideration in the form of land, livestock, clothes, money, or some combination of that.

When Jan arrived in New Amsterdam, there were no immigration issues, and it was still part of his country. It was 1650, and he was twenty-three years old. He traveled to New Amsterdam and remained indentured for three years. He then received land, clothes, some money, and livestock. Jan settled in Bergen, New Jersey, and farmed the land he received. He then sold that farm and moved to the outskirts of today's Flatbush. The farm he purchased is located within today's Prospect Park.

He married Annaken Hendericks, who was also a Dutch immigrant from Doesburg, Holland. They were married in 1650 while Jan was still indentured. Annaken was born in 1620, while Jan was born in 1627, making her seven years older. They had four children together: Gerritje Janse, Aris Janse, Marittje Janse, and Aert

Janse. Sometime after the fourth child was born, Annaken passed away. Jan then married his second wife, Dieber Cornelis, and had one child with her—Jacob Janse Vanderbilt. She brought along two children from her previous marriage. After she passed away, Jan married Magdalena Hanse and had one more son with her, Aris Janse Vanderbilt.

Our story today branches at Jan's third marriage and to the child from that marriage, Jan Janse Vanderbilt.

By the time Jan was married, he had already officially changed his name from van Der Bilt, meaning from the Village of Bilt, to Vanderbilt, a single family name. This he passed on to his progeny, including Aris Janse who was born in 1653 on the farm in Flatbush.

Aris and his stepbrother Jacob worked hard on their father's land, and they bought more land for investment with the help of loans, mortgages, and by working hard to pay off those loans. They succeeded in buying more land in the Flatbush area. Eventually, the two brothers accumulated close to one hundred acres of land in Flatbush and more land across the Hudson in New Jersey.

It was the same year that the Dutch built a fortification in the lower part of the city that ran from the Hudson River to the East River. The landscape of lower Manhattan today looks nothing like the landscape that originally mapped the island. What is today's Greenwich Street in the west was where land met the Hudson River. On the east side, where today's Pearl Street is located, is where the East River used to border.

The Dutch built a wall at the edge of that, which ran between the two rivers that defined the east and west shorelines and was called The Belt. It was called *Het Cingle* by the Dutch.

When the British conquered the city and Governor Peter Stuyvesant surrendered New Amsterdam to the British, it happened without any fight by the Dutch, and the Dutch colonists were allowed to stay peacefully. These included Jans and the rest of the Vanderbilts. Their citizenry was transferred from being that of Dutch to being English subjects.

Once the area was occupied by the British, the wall along *Her Cingle* was demolished, which had come to be known as Wall Street. The land below it, including areas of Battery Park today, was then reclaimed from the sea and built upon. Reclamation was also conducted on the East River embankment and on the Hudson as well. After years of reclamation and reshaping the island, the southern part of Manhattan that we know today finally came to be the shape it is as you see now.

Aris spent some time learning to speak and cultivate the land, and then joined his father, elder brothers, and stepbrother working the farm and helping the family put food on the table. The family was not as poor as some were in those days, but they lived hand to mouth and spent all their money on buying more landed property.

Aris eventually married Hillitje and continued working on the farm. Together, they had eleven children, including Jacobus Vanderbilt (named after Aris' brother), which is the line that leads to the topic of this book. Jacobus was born

January 24, 1692. As the Flatbush area offered no more land for purchase, Aris turned his sights to other islands around the New York harbor. He found vacant land on an island that had been named after the Dutch Parliament, *Staaten Eylaandt*, by Henry Hudson. Hudson, although English by birth, was sailing under the Dutch flag when he came to the New World.

Aris purchased about eighty acres of land on the southern side *Staaten Eylaandt*, now known as New Dorp. It was a magnificent spread of land with clear views of the bay to the east and mainland New Jersey and Sandy Hook Bay to the south. Most of the acreage he purchased was densely forested. It is now part of the landscape that holds the remains of the Vanderbilt family, including Commodore Vanderbilt.

Jacobus, or Jacob for short, married Neltje Denyse and made a deal with his father to buy sixty-eight acres of the New Dorp land for a relatively low price of three hundred pounds. He had no cash to pay for it, so he struck a mortgage on the property, which his father held. As for his other properties, Aris divided them among his children. He died soon afterward, releasing Jacob's liabilities.

The land that Jacob bought was densely wooded. he cut down the timber to clear his land and used some of it to build a home for himself and Neltje. Here the Vanderbilts of the seventeenth century lived a sparse life of minimalism and frugality. The home they built was merely a shelter from the elements, the children shared beds and clothes, and the family ate what they harvested and slaughtered.

Jacob was unable to work all of the land, and they saved much of their meager earnings to buy a slave.

By 1720, Jacob had a few more slaves on his farm, but he was not a typical slave master. He worked with them and treated them relatively well. As he increased his enterprise, he was able to buy more land next to the original sixty-eight acres he had purchased from Aris—fifty acres that bordered his own land. By this point, he had twelve children, and everyone worked the land.

Among the twelve was Jacob Vanderbilt II, who would become Commodore Vanderbilt's grandfather.

It was around this time that the once Protestant Van der Bilt converted to Moravian teachings. The long line of Dutch Vanderbilts had been broken by Jacob II when he was the first of his family to have a wife who was not Dutch. Jacob II married Mary Sprague whose father was from New England and of British stock.

Jacob II had two children with Mary: Eleanor Johnson and Cornelius Vanderbilt (Sr). Cornelius was born August 28, 1764, in Rahway, New Jersey.

By this point, the British had already imposed the Sugar Act on the colonies. It was the beginning of taxation without representation in the colonies, and the thirteen existing colonies at this time were starting to rumble beneath the surface with revolt.

At the time of his birth, Cornelius Vanderbilt, Sr. was part of a well-known family. The Vanderbilts were upstanding members of the

Staten Island community. They were bilingual, spoke Dutch and English, and were all senior members of the Moravian church. They had been involved in the building of *Irene*, the ship that sailed between New York and Holland to rescue Moravians persecuted for religious beliefs.

The population of the New York city area around 1700 when Jacob I was born was about six thousand. By the time Cornelius Sr. was born, it had doubled to twelve thousand. The American Revolution was around the corner, and Cornelius Senior was about two years old when Jacob II passed away. Much of the land that had been in the family in the New Dorp area was slowly whittled away and given to other children and relatives. The prosperity that was to be enjoyed at birth was slowly dwindling, and two years later Mary Vanderbilt passed away, leaving Cornelius Sr. an orphan just four years old.

Those who had stayed near Jacob II during his lifetime and managed to scrape a living off of him were now running in the other direction not wanting to take Senior and raise him. He was finally taken in by an uncle who owned the Rose and Crown Tavern, which served British soldiers who had come to occupy the area. King George's son, Prince William Henry, frequently stayed here on his deployment to the colonies. Sir William Howe, the British general, also camped here for most of the war.

Senior worked the tables, took out the trash, and mopped the floors from the time he was five. He wasn't sent to school and was illiterate all his life. The experience of being put to work in such harsh conditions at such a tender age altered his trajectory and made him bitter with a rough demeanor. He grew up to be a man who had no patience for anyone else and was always negative in his outlook. He passed a lot of this on to his son later in life.

By the time he was an adult, Senior did not get any part of his father's vast acreage in New Dorp. It had all been given to relatives and later sold. He left New Dorp when he was sixteen and old enough to strike out on his own, but he only got as far away as Port Richmond on the north side of the island, just across from today's Bayonne.

Here, Senior got a job as a sailor. He was to sail periaugers, a thirty-foot, two-masted flatboat that carried produce up to Upper New York Harbor around lower Manhattan and Jersey City. This area was busy in the 1700s and early 1800s with exports increasing and immigrants arriving. By the time Senior started plying these routes, the British Navy dominated the scene.

He was a hard worker. He kept his head down, not wanting to get into trouble for anything and just kept doing his job. He saved every penny, not wasting any of it on drink or anything fancy. In time, he saved enough to get his own periauger and was able to now ply the same route for all the profit. When he turned twenty-three in 1787, Senior met and wed Phoebe Hand. The two were polar opposites, but Senior was a handsome man, and Phoebe fell in love with him on sight.

She was also of British ancestry just like Senior's mother, and she, too, had been orphaned at a very young age. In her case, however, she was educated and had been surrounded by educated people. This union had tremendous benefit for Senior, as she guided him on what to do and how to expand his business.

Phoebe was raised by the family of a Protestant minister in Rahway, New Jersey, and she brought that culture and piety to the home of Cornelius Vanderbilt, Sr.

Chapter 4 Cornelius

Senior had worked hard before the marriage and worked harder afterward but this time with more direction and purpose. When he was young, he did not drink or gamble, but as he grew older and after getting married, he took to drinking rum. Phoebe, however, had a hand in keeping all that to a minimum and being frugal with the family's finances.

Once married, they rented a small farm and house that overlooked the water in Port Richmond, and with her great stewardship and his hard work, they saved enough to buy that farm. It wasn't just Senior's earnings that went toward buying it but also a lot of her inheritance.

Senior tilled the farm, and they had four children while he was still running the periauger service up and down the harbor. The produce from the farm was enough to feed the small family of six. Life was not easy but certainly a lot better than what Senior had faced after his mother's passing.

They named their children Mary, after Senior's mother; Jacob after his father; Charlotte after Phoebe's sister, and Cornelius Vanderbilt I, who was born May 27, 1794. The war was now over and the British mostly gone—at least the soldiers were—and General George Washington was now President George Washington. More Vanderbilt children were to come, but that would happen in the next house the family moved to.

In late 1795 once Cornelius Junior was a year old, Senior decided that it was time to move to a larger home. The Vanderbilts sold their waterfront farm and moved to a house overlooking the Narrows and Brooklyn on the east side of the island. Here they had five more children. Not all of them survived, but in sequence, they were Phoebe, named after Senior's wife; Jane; Eleanor; Jacob; and Phoebe. The last two were born and named for two other Vanderbilt children who had died young.

Even though the house was more expensive than the last and stretched the family's expenses to the brink, it was not a bad investment in any way. Due to Phoebe's expert hand and constant frugal ways, she raised all her children and her husband with the guidance and love of a saint. The kindness of a preacher's daughter was something that saw the family through all the ups and downs that raising a big family entailed.

In retrospect, this home was worth the extra sweat and toil because of its great influence on Junior. The house sat a mere two hundred feet from the beach and offered a first-class view of the various ships that sailed up the Narrows into New York Harbor.

As young Cornelius sat by the window and looked out, the view was never the same two days in a row. He could see sails of navy frigates and European freighters as well as schooners and brigantines. By the time he was four, he knew what all the ships were and where they were coming from. He had a head for the colors and sails.

Junior knew that his father sailed up and down the harbor. He couldn't wait to do the same. It created a desire in his heart and sharpened his will to do more than just sit around watching the boats sail by. Records indicate that Senior was only able to launch and offer his services by using a few periaugers that he bought and hired other sailors to operate. That is how they made their money and paid the bills. Rumors suggest that Senior had a ferry service and passed that down to Junior, but this cannot be confirmed. It seems more likely that Senior hauled produce and did not ferry passengers.

Nonetheless, the business of hauling goods and produce went well, and the Vanderbilts did not have significant problems while Junior was growing up. The beach offered more than just a view of magnificent boats. It also offered many activities during the summer months. As the weather became hotter, children would find their way to the shores and play. Young Vanderbilt loved riding horses and would do so without a saddle even at a young age.

He was able to tame wild horses by the time he was seven and ride along the eastern shore of Tompkinsville.

He was naturally athletic, which made him a natural at running, horse riding, and even boxing in his later years. The outdoors and everything athletic came to define Junior's preteen years and even his young adulthood to a lesser degree. He also had a sharp mind and soon wanted to make money in any way that he could.

The young Vanderbilt was rough and tumble. Although he was handsome and charming, he did not have any problem with getting in the dirt to beat up someone. There was nothing refined or gentlemanly about him, which he freely admitted.

By the age of eleven when his elder brother died, Junior was now the eldest boy in the family, and it fell on him to help his father with ferrying. He did this gladly since it called upon two of his dearest attributes—to make money and sail. He started off taking one of his father's periaugers and going up to the Battery (south of Manhattan) and charging customers of opportunity that came along. He made a few pennies every day, and was doing what he loved.

He was significantly much more daring than his father and would make many trips each day if the wind and tide allowed.

As he became more familiar with sailing and the bay area, Senior hired another boy, and the two of them would take the vessel out on more runs, and he would get paid a decent wage by his father. He made more money now than before, and the work was more consistent.

But it wasn't as good as what he learned to do next.

South of Staten Island between Raritan Bay and Sandy Hook the ground rises up just under the surf. Most of the pilots who came up the lower bay knew a sandy shoal is here and avoided it. Sometimes, however, cargo ships had inexperienced pilots and ran aground. When this happened, the law indicated that salvage operations could be conducted, and the salvage operator had all rights to the salvaged goods.

Junior and his father would constantly keep their eye on Sandy Hook and rush down to a disabled ship and unload goods and then sell what they salvaged. In many cases, Junior made more money through salvage work than with his daily operations.

Chapter 5 Enterprise and Negotiation

Junior had two things going for him at this point in his life: (1) he had an innate desire to do something with ships. He absolutely loved anything that moved on the water, and (2) he wanted to make money in any way that he could. Considerable evidence indicates his desire to make money for both the sake of living an opulent life—a life that money and wealth can buy in terms of material accumulation—as well as the power that entails.

The United States at that time had no railroads or steamships, and the Industrial Revolution had not yet occurred.

The Industrial Revolution had just altered the way America went about its business. Until just after the American Revolution, productivity had increased, and textiles were now a major export as was cotton. The period in New York after the war saw a rapid increase in population. The increase in activity in and around the harbor bode well for the Vanderbilts, and their on-demand ferrying business did well. The only limiting factor in all this was Senior. He did just enough to get by and would not work harder than was absolutely necessary.

Junior saw the world differently. He wasn't blinded by the pain of a rough childhood. He had his mother and father and to a certain extent his brothers and sisters who were always there in a safe and secure environment. His mother had given him the start he needed, and he was clear in his thinking and ambitions. He didn't know how he was going to do it. He just knew he would be successful.

As any young man thinks, Junior wanted to do what he knew best, and this was the Upper and Lower Bay—where he knew how to maneuver his little craft and get goods and people to the many different shores that lined the harbor.

As he was still a minor, he was unable to leave home and make it on his own. So he came up with a plan to advance himself. He was after all sixteen years old and ready to hit the world just as his father had done when he left the tavern. In this case, however, it was also his mother who couldn't bear to see her eldest boy flung far away from her care. Junior recognized the leverage he had. He wanted more but only had his youth and strength to trade at this stage of his life. It was the first evidence of his ability to want something, work at it, and then execute the plan needed to be successful.

He was quite the negotiator and told his parents that he wanted to earn a living on one of the boats that were sailing out, and that he was old enough to be able to do it. He seemed to try to convince them that letting him go on one of these ships would enable him to make the money he wanted.

His mother strenuously objected but could see that he was determined. His father, who didn't think it was such a bad idea, didn't acquiesce mainly because he wanted his son close to him to help with work and because he knew Phoebe would be upset. What they both didn't know is that they were being played.

Junior then told his parents that if they didn't want to let him go at least they should loan him $100 (this was circa 1812, so that value is approximately $2,000 today) to buy his own periauger. Compared to permitting him to board a transatlantic cargo ship, the periauger idea was significantly more palatable. Both parents agreed.

They did, however, attach some conditions to the loan. The first was that they shared his profits for the rest of the year in addition to paying back the $100. The second was that he had to clear an acre of land that the family owned.

Junior agreed. His plan had gone off without a hitch. He got to work on the land and within a month had it cleared out. Then he bought his own periauger. It is said that the day he got into his own vessel he could feel the exhilaration. He fancied himself a captain of one of those ships he saw sailing up the Narrows. It was what he had wanted to do from as far back as he could recall.

This experience set the path for the rest of his life. It began to occur to Junior that he could get anything he wanted if he just desired it and then set his own brand of negotiations.

He had displayed a significant ability to negotiate, but it was not the kind of negotiation we think of in our daily life. Junior had the innate ability to foresee the path to getting what he wanted, and he would lay the strategy so that his counterparts would follow like lambs to the slaughter. In time, as he matured, so did his ability to negotiate until it took on a competitive shade, even being unscrupulous at times. As time passed, he only got better at it, and all he wanted to do was to get the next goal and the next pot of gold.

Then came his next challenge. At this point, he was in debt for $100. As much as the loan was from parent to child, he saw it as a ball chained to his foot. His first job was to pay off this debt and give the profits to his parents for the following year.

He paid off the $100 within six weeks and then in the course of the year netted his benefactors a shade over a thousand dollars in profit. This was the path to his second lesson in life. With the burden of debt on his shoulders, he had to make every fare and fill every last square inch of space on his periauger every day that he was sailing.

He learned about capacity utilization at sixteen in the same way that MBAs learn it in Ivy League B-schools except he learned it on the job. He would sail in the foulest of weather and on the calmest of days when it was enticing to just lay back on the beach and enjoy the sun on one's face or go to the local tavern. Junior would have none of that. When conditions were bad, he would sail; when the weather was good, he would double his efforts. His philosophy was to keep his asset working at all times to generate the most amount of income. Keeping his transportation full was more important than the price that was levied on the customer. In later years, he would have the same strategy when dealing with Rockefeller's oil coming out of Titusville. He would give a 30 percent discount to the average price so that Rockefeller would fill his trains rather than letting them run at partial capacity.

At sixteen, Junior proved himself to be a tough teenager. The shores of Staten Island were a nice place to relax, especially in summer, but the ferry business was not something that was filled with niceties and fun. It was a cutthroat business. Many of the fights that Junior had were fights with other competitors who didn't like that he was always making money while they weren't. Some of the strategies they did not like were that young Cornelius would undercut the prices he charged someone just so that he could keep his hull full.

They also didn't like that he would charge above-market rates when it was raining or the surf was choppy. He took risks that others wouldn't and charged more for it. Junior had the innate ability to understand pricing and charging mechanisms. He understood the equations of supply and demand and realized that a full hull at a cheaper price was better than a partially empty hull at a more expensive price. This strategy was something he also applied later in life when he ran ships down to Nicaragua.

He became involved in his Southern shipping business when he wanted to take advantage of the Gold Rush. When East Coast residents were paying almost a thousand dollars to cross the plains, Junior devised a way to sail them down to Nicaragua, where he could find a relatively narrow part of the isthmus, and then load his customers on a land journey to the Pacific coast. He would then ship them on another boat up to California. It saved each passenger time and hundreds of dollars. He had undercut all the stagecoach businesses that were going from both coasts and the other ships that were rounding the Cape in South America to make the trip.

Operators who were losing big money decided to pay him $50,000 per month just to get him to stop his service. How many businesspeople can one name who would be paid to stop doing what they were doing? That is how efficient he was at doing what he did.

He then developed his next skill in the harbor area. After spending the first year running the ferry service and paying off his parents' capital and profits, he zeroed in on his second boat. He borrowed the money necessary, but this time he only borrowed a quarter of the amount he needed instead of the full amount. He had already saved all the rest. His second boat was piloted by two other sailors whom he hired. He was notoriously vicious with the schedule. He never left it up to the sailors as to when they would sail. He decided. They sailed whenever he told them to, and he would fill up two vessels every day regardless of the weather. If the sailors were not doing a good job or hesitated, he would fire them. If a fight broke out between him and the sailors, he would take them on, and he never lost a fistfight with one of these rough and tough men.

He paid off the debt owed on the second boat within two weeks, and then it dawned on him that there was enough capacity in the harbor to warrant even more boats. By the time he turned eighteen, he had four periaugers, all of them were paid for in full, and they were working across the water on a daily basis. His loads were always at capacity. At this point, he started to calculate that it was time for a larger boat.

Junior realized that periaugers weren't the best craft for New York harbor. In the fall and early winter, it was windy, and the periauger, which does not have a keel, was not the best vessel to maneuver the waters. When a vessel has no keel, it can't control the tendency of the boat to slip sideways in the direction of the prevailing wind. It was hard to maneuver, and there was an overreliance on wind and tide conditions. That was one of the main reasons why strong currents dictated that periaugers would only sail in when the basin filled with the incoming tide and sailed out when the basin drained at low tide.

He decided that a sloop would work best for him. He zeroed in on one that was sixty-five feet in length. With its keel, single headsail, and fore and aft rig, he concluded that it would be a better craft to use on even the harshest days. He was already out on the water more often than most periauger sailors on the bay, and now with the sloop, he would do even better. He commissioned the ship in 1813 and set sail that summer when he was nineteen years old.

What made it even better was that the deep centerboard hull allowed him to make many more trips between Manhattan and Staten Island because he was no longer at the mercy of the tide and wind.

He christened the sloop *Swiftsure* after the British warship. Since he was a young boy, he had fancied himself as a British navy captain, and this was his first opportunity to live that fantasy.

For all his desire to captain a boat in the British navy, he was not in any way loyal to the navy, the British, the Americans, or the Dutch. He was in it for himself. He didn't care whom he worked with or what flag flew high above him. He was more interested in the tangible effects of the world around him than the abstract matters of state and loyalty.

Chapter 6 1812

Napoleon took power in France in the wake of the French Revolution. He quickly moved to become emperor by 1804. Within four years, he had waged numerous battles against other European countries and conquered a sizeable portion of Europe.

More importantly, Bonaparte had the hearts and minds of the French. The British were on the run in many places, and Napoleon defeated the British in several sea battles.

The British constantly needed to replenish their ranks with sailors and started to look to America. In the Treaty of Paris, which was signed after the American Revolution, Britain had agreed to hand over the forts they had occupied. Almost two dozen years had passed since the signing of the treaty, but the forts had still not been returned. The British were using those forts to blockade the French from trading with the United States. The French were allies of the newly independent colony since it was because of the French that Washington was able to defeat Lord Cornwallis.

The British army was also capturing, or "impressing," local sailors and putting them in the British navy to fight Napoleon. Both of these actions were an act of war.

It all came to a boil on the eve of 1812, and the busy trade all along the waters of New York's harbor dwindled to almost nothing. Between the blockade at sea that halted trade and the indiscriminate capture of sailors, New York activity had come to a halt.

The government had decided that they would not stand for it, and along with the battle that ensued between America and Britain, the army started to build batteries and walls with canons along the harbor.

The Army Corps of Engineers was called in to build the necessary walls, embankments, and other defensive structures to protect the harbor and New York City. While all the other periauger boat sailors and captains of the other ferries had slowed down during the blockade, Junior was one of the few who started offering contracts to the U.S. Army to ferry men, equipment, and supplies to various areas of construction in the bay.

What had been a downfall for most of the sailors and ferry operators was actually a tremendous opportunity for the industrious Vanderbilt. During the war, it has been said that Junior was the only one who was willing to exchange passage for payment regardless of the weather. He continuously kept his boats full during the lean years of the War of 1812.

Even though few sailors were active in the harbor, and all who did worked for Vanderbilt in one way or another, their lean years became his first golden opportunity. When others went out of business, he bought their boats and expanded his fleet with the contracts he received from the army.

With more boats, a secure contract, and few competitors, Junior started to see what it was like to have a meaningful amount of money. He started to spend it on loose women who were present in areas with sailors. It was at this time that he started to behave this way himself. He was not a drunkard, as he didn't want to lose his senses or his money, so he wasn't interested in drink or gambling. It was always about women, especially those who were cheap. This activity excited him, and it didn't stop even after he married or could afford significantly better.

He had become a businessman by this time and was far more astute than his father. The Dutch Van Der Bilt genes he shared with his grandfather, his uncles, and great grandfather who had worked hard and developed the lands in Flatbush and New Dorp, between which he sailed his growing fleet, had a lot in common. He was indeed a businessman by instinct, and he knew how to apply muscle and brain to the same problem. That ability to think about, take advantage of, and work hard at anything and everything he did brought success to him in every undertaking in which he became involved.

By this point, Junior had developed into a strong man with a purpose. He found that making money was significantly easier for him than his father. He also started to realize that making money was a state of mind that absorbed him. He no longer had anything or anyone more important to him than the concept of making money.

This subconscious and superconscious (at the same time) state of existence turns every endeavor into materialistic pursuit. There was nothing bad about this. In fact, it made him supereffective and superefficient in all activities.

He had upgraded from the periauger to the sloop. It was not that he was a trained seaman. He learned on his own and observed. His state of mind was that he was always looking to improve himself. In the case of the upgrades, he realized that the boat that he wanted would do better than the boat he had, and that would translate to more money. For as long as his father was ferrying people across the bay, he never once taught of trading up. He was happy where he was and did just enough to get by. Junior was significantly different. His ability to trade up was inherent and persistent.

Also important at this time were his relationships with the opposite sex. He was a transactional person. It didn't matter if he was trading with sailors or brothel workers, it was always just a transaction—nothing more and nothing less.

This transactional attitude with all things that he undertook and his ability to always trade up meant that Junior was always a person in search of a better deal in return for something that he didn't want. His later dealings with Rockefeller also exemplified this trait.

Of all the people he dealt with, from his father down to his children and all the ruffians and sailors on the shore, he showed only some form of deference to his mother and would listen to her if she lectured him. The same could not be said for his father or the woman he would soon marry. From the time before he proposed and married her all the way to the point when they lived in different houses later in life, he was never faithful to her. Their relationship was no more transactional than the fleeting relationships he had with his most favored lady of the brothel.

As 1812 drew to a close and the war still raged on, Junior was working hard at his business and playing hard at the seafront brothels of Manhattan. From all accounts, it didn't matter how much he played. He always appeared at work bright and early and ready to put in a sixteen-hour day. One activity never took away from the other.

Chapter 7 Converging Heritage

The Vanderbilt family lived all across Staten Island and Queens. Junior's grandfather, Jacob II, had a large holding of land in the New Dorp area. Aside from Cornelius Sr., grandpa Vanderbilt also had a daughter, Eleanor Vanderbilt, who was Senior's sister. She married a man by the name of Nathaniel Johnson. The couple had a son, Nathaniel Johnson II. which made Nathanial Johnson II and Junior cousins. Nathanial Johnson II married a lady named Elizabeth Hand. Phoebe's maiden name was also Hand. (Phoebe and Elizabeth were cousins.)

Nathanial Johnson II and Elizabeth Hand had a few children, one of whom was born in 1795 and named Sophia Johnson. That makes Sophia related to Junior twice over. Through his father, they are second cousins (Junior's aunt's granddaughter). Then again through his mother, they are second cousins.

This proximity in the family tree was enough for Junior's mother to reject the union. It was one of the few times that Junior refused to take his mother's council, and he persisted. She had a sultry and mesmerizing look with a hit of Phoebe's features that attracted him. As for Sophia, she was attracted to Junior's height, muscle tone, and charming good looks.

Even though Junior was enjoying the waterfront brothels, he still needed a transaction to get his family and a stable of sons lined up. Getting married to the prettiest girl on the northern shore in Port Richmond was also a feather in his cap.

It turned out that his mother was right. The bloodlines were too close to escape the effects of a consanguineous relationship. One of their children would later be born with epilepsy, which Junior could not tolerate.

After a relentless campaign to obtain his parents' approval, he eventually received it, and the happy couple were married December 19, 1813. The War of 1812 was still being fought, and the construction and military activities that still continued in the harbor caused Junior to continue working 16-hour days. He was back at work the day after the wedding.

From this point, it would serve us well to refer to Junior as Vanderbilt.

The couple got busy with building a family. They moved into a rented house not far from Senior and Phoebe. That move was intentional because it allowed Phoebe to look in on them and also to keep her new daughter-in-law company.

A string of children soon followed, as was the tradition of the time. In all, there were thirteen children, almost born annually. In sequence, the children were Phoebe Jane in the middle of 1814, Ethelinda in 1817, William Henry in 1821, Emily Elmira in 1823, Sophia Johnson in 1825, Maria Louisa in 1827, Frances Lavinia in 1828, Cornelius Jeremiah in 1830, Maria Alicia in 1834, Catherine Juliet in 1836, and George Washington in 1839.

From all accounts, Vanderbilt and Sophia had a strained relationship. His transactional nature only saw her as the mother of his children. He never consulted her on his business or his plans. That he left to his mother and sometimes his father. His parents had continued to be his partners in the business starting from the first boat for which they loaned him the $100. All the subsequent boats also had their names on it even though his money paid for them.

Sophia's name was not on any of them.

She would look after the children while he was out working and strolling the waterfront. He would also not bring money home. He had her on a very tight budget to feed the increasing number of children, while he spent most of the money in expanding the business.

In part, this was done with Phoebe's approval. By the time the War of 1812 was over, Vanderbilt had added three more ships to his fleet. Two were schooners, and one was a larger sloop. These were launched in the summer of 1814 just after the Treaty of Ghent was signed officially ending the War of 1812. The timing could not be more perfect, as the harbor came back to life with more trade coming in, and the first pick of the business went to the man with the larger boats. Vanderbilt had swooped in at the right time and anticipated the upswing in trade in New York.

While he was putting money away for the expansion of his fleet, Sophia was managing the budget at home and making sure he always had a warm meal when he came home.

Even though money was always tight, they moved into a larger house a few years after the War ended and continued to have more children. Sophia continued to try to earn her husband's confidence but to no avail. She didn't give up hope, though, and continued to respect Phoebe and Senior, who came around as often as they could to see the grandchildren and make sure that Sophia was taking care of things.

With a number of the original periaugers still in operation and a couple of schooners and sloops plying the shores of upper and lower New York Harbor, Vanderbilt started to set his sights on routes farther up and down the Eastern seaboard.

He would still get into fights with other sailors and boat operators and always win. His reputation all along the shoreline was that of a tough character who needed to be respected. For lack of a better term, he beat his competitors into submission.

As the revenues went up, so did Vanderbilt's propensity to expand. He had no intention of staying stagnant, and now he was seriously considering a new venture. He would expand his routes beyond the bay area and started sending his ships up the Hudson River carrying grain to the mills and flour on the return trip. Now he wanted to venture to the south, but since he was not experienced in this area, he decided to take on his brother-in-law as a partner.

Charlotte Vanderbilt had married Captain John DeForest. He was a seasoned sailor and captain who had years of experience sailing up and down the Eastern coastline from Boston to New York and down to Charleston and Savannah.

Vanderbilt and DeForest partnered on a large schooner they named after Charlotte. The *Charlotte* was designed specifically to ply the open waters and navigate the rougher seas of the Atlantic. It was the largest vessel that Vanderbilt had ever owned. Captain DeForest and Vanderbilt made the maiden voyage down to Savannah in the fall of 1815, where he taught Vanderbilt all the theory and practice of open sea sailing. It was an eye-opening event for Vanderbilt and something he realized that he had wanted to do ever since the days of sitting in his parents' house across the Narrows as a toddler.

He was now on the open ocean, and the feeling was exhilarating, but he was there to make money, and he never forgot that. They reached Savannah and dropped off their maiden cargo and started their voyage back up north. Vanderbilt was able to learn and was quick at grasping the skills he needed to pilot his new boat.

On the way, they moored in Chesapeake Bay and filled the empty cargo bays with oysters. When they returned to New York, they sold the cargo for $1,500. This was in addition to the money they made from the maiden cargo they dropped off in Savannah.

In another example of profit at all costs and under all conditions, Vanderbilt displayed his ability to extract opportunity out of all situations. A typical captain would have just quickly sailed back to port to get back to his family or visit one of the taverns onshore. For Vanderbilt, it was always about business first.

When there weren't goods to ferry or passengers to put up with (he despised carrying passengers but did so only to maximize his haul), he turned to fishing. He would dispatch all his vessels up the Hudson across Long Island Sound and into the bay to catch shad. He would have the *Charlotte* go into deeper waters for a better catch. He would get other boatmen to convoy together and lay nets off the New Jersey coast and catch whatever they could. They could then come back to the docks and sell their catch to the wholesalers. He was never idle. If he didn't work sixteen hours a day, he would become grumpy, and Sophia would hear about it when he came home.

After returning to port, he assigned Captain DeForest to the southern routes on the *Charlotte* and sold all but one of the periaugers—the first one he bought. He also kept the other sloops and schooners. In all, he now had five vessels and four sailors and himself working them. They all worked twelve- to sixteen-hour days, and every penny that was brought in went to paying wages and saving for future expansion, while Sophia sat at home dutifully looking after Vanderbilt and raising their children.

Not once in all the time they were married did he ever update her on the business or ask for her opinion even though she was more educated than he was. He was almost illiterate and only able to read a little and write even less. He knew his numbers and how to calculate the shipping number he needed and the cost of money and the interest that was levied on his borrowings, but that was it.

Sophia had the patience of a saint. She waited for the time he would give her more attention and trust her advice, but she knew it was not her place to speak. She paid dutiful reverence to her in-laws and continued to serve in the best maternal role she could for her children. The more he excluded her from decision-making and sought Phoebe's counsel, the more she longed, but the moment she hoped for never came.

The only thing she had from the marriage was the thirteen children whom she loved dearly. She was a dutiful wife that he had married because she looked like his mother, but he never gave her the attention she deserved. In her last days, she remained in the mansion he built for her on Staten Island and died while he lived in the townhouse in Manhattan. She had chosen not to move to Manhattan.

Chapter 8 Opportunist

When you consider almost every wealthy entrepreneur, you will find that they have no loyalty to a single idea. Look at every robber baron or titan of the gilded age and you will find that to be true. Wall Street traders call it "not falling in love with a stock." In other words, you do not find one product and stay with it until you die. Bill Gates started with DOS and went to Windows. Steve Jobs started with the iMac and went to the iPhone. Carnegie started with iron bridges and went to steel, and just to make the point, Rockefeller started with produce and went into refining petroleum.

What all of them had in common was that they were opportunists. An opportunist in this sense is not about fleecing others when the opportunity comes up but to take opportunities of an enterprise when it arises in front of them. A blind man and an unfocused man will not see it and be inclined to pass on it.

In Vanderbilt's case, he saw vessels and ships pass in front of him every day, morning and night, and had ever since he could remember, and he dreamed of becoming wealthy, but then the time came to give it all up for an opportunity that was much greater than his seafaring vessels, and he gave it up after just a moment's thought. He sold his entire fleet to take advantage of the new form of transportation in America—trains.

His unemotional move from the boats he added one at a time and sailed each one had no bearing on this emotion or his nostalgia. He was not loyal to boating; he didn't fall in love with it. When the time came to trade them for something more, he did.

An opportunist needs certain characteristics to be able to make use of the opportunities that come his way. He must be pulled to them, not pushed away. Carnegie, Rockefeller, and Vanderbilt did not push their initial businesses away because it was hard to do. They didn't hesitate even for a moment because what they were doing was hard or causing them grief or even because they were failing at it. They didn't get pushed from what they were doing in search of an easier alternative. No matter how hard it was to sail the periaugers on the unpredictable waters of New York's harbor or how difficult it was for Carnegie to build his bridges and do so on time or how hard it was for Rockefeller to increase sales of his produce, they never left the business they had in hand because it was hard. They left it because they had something more that interested them.

Opportunists also do not fall in love with what they are doing and let an opportunity for advancement sail past them. If you see an opportunity that is better than what you are doing, then it's time to take what you have from this one and apply it to the next.

Opportunits do not confuse knowledge and skill for academics. Vanderbilt did not read many books in his life. In fact, it wouldn't be too much of a stretch to conclude that he did not read a single book in his life. He knew how to read a little, and Sophia taught him a little, and so did his mother. If there were things he didn't know, he relied on them to read it to him and even explain it as needed. His role model, Senior, was also fairly illiterate, and he, too, relied on his wife to relate the contents of mortgages or documents that needed his mark. What he lacked in academic schooling and formal education, however, he made up for in intellect.

The same can be said of Carnegie who only went to school until the age of thirteen, similar to Rockefeller, who only grazed past schooling for a short time as well—just enough to read. What all these men did know, however, was how to manage numbers in their heads. That was important in understanding what was important in their business.

Academics levy an opportunistic cost on the student. They get to learn all the theory they can possibly spread themselves offer in return they get to learn none of it in real life. They lose the ability to adapt their mind to realities and instead rely on formulas and rules. Vanderbilt relied on neither. You could say that he was a realist.

Opportunists are also humble. It is ironic to include Vanderbilt in any list that is derived from humility. The picture that his life paints does not seem to project that quality, but in fact he was humble. He did not see any job to be beneath him, and he did not see any fare to be beyond his effort. In other words, he would do the job as long as he had the time to do it and if he promised it.

When he wanted the seed capital to purchase his first periauger and managed to convince his parents, he had to clear a plot of land to make it ready to farm. The land had brush and trees, rocks and debris, and it took considerable work to clear it. He did not have the money to pay additional workers. When he set out to do the job, he did not see how much work was in front of him but only that there was a benefit at the end of the job—and it wasn't a hundred dollars. His benefit was the freedom to have his own enterprise. That made the effort at hand a small price to pay.

Vanderbilt's opportunistic ink was prevalent. He was colored by it in all aspects of his undertaking. It was also part of the reason he seemed transactional in all that he undertook.

From his dalliances with waterfront women to his seemingly cold relationship with his wife and even his casual relationship with the people who came to work for him, he was evidently transactional. It was always about the transaction—this for that. He had no love for anything in his life—not his wife or his children. His only one true love may have been his mother, but even that may have been tinged with the ink of transaction. He trusted his mother's counsel and relied on her acumen for the business decisions he made. Even that, though, was a transaction.

There was no opportunity on the harbor that he did not try—from moving goods up and down the river, harbor, and eastern shoreline to fishing in the off days and even using his smaller vessels to sail up to ships and act as a delivery service for whatever they wanted from shore to be delivered to them, and even applied if what they wanted were services from the nearby brothels.

He certainly had a powerful imagination with what he could do with his vessels. That was how he was able to return the investment to his parents in six weeks and then give them a thousand dollars in profit within one year.

By 1820, the war had become a distant memory, and trade had started to expand rapidly. The growth before the war was admirable, but after the war it was even greater. The effects of the Industrial Revolution and the demand for goods that were coming out of America, between its natural resources, from fur to timber, for finished goods from textiles to ships, and in agriculture from corn to cotton, made New York Harbor alive with activity.

With the increasing business of the banks in New York, it was certain that ships that came from Southern ports would stop in New York so that bankers' agents could sight the cargo that was being exported. That meant that regardless of where the product was coming from or going to, it was more likely now that it had to stop in New York for banking and insurance purposes.

There would even be ship-to-shore transfers of goods coming from the South aboard vessels that were suited to ply the coast but not suited to sail the waters of the deep Atlantic. These ships would unload their cargo at the port and then sail back down the coast, while larger ships would load those items and then set sail for Europe.

Vanderbilt would often provide his services for all these activities, including the transfer of cargo from the ships that had no place to berth. They would anchor at sea and transfer the goods aboard their smaller ships to be unloaded at the port.

From transporting all kinds of goods across all the ports up and down the coast to contractual services and impromptu services, nothing was too good or too difficult for Vanderbilt. Within a few short years of taking ownership of the *Charlotte*, Vanderbilt was known in every port from New England to Georgia.

This was the height of his business as he knew it. Then came the next phase of his life—something that only an opportunist could see. Through the 1700s and the early part of the 1800s, most of the traffic that dotted New York Harbor was powered by the wind, tide, and oars. The power of the vessel was determined by how many masts it supported and how large a sail those masts flew.

Vanderbilt grew up seeing those sails and colors that stretched from the topsail to the jib in the fore to the mainsail and the aft jib. Now, a man by the name of Livingston had developed a new beast—the steam engine—with its boilers that burned pine wood to heat large amounts of water and use that steam to turn wheels that functioned as perpetual paddles.

When they first started appearing in the Narrows, Vanderbilt didn't think much of them. He pejoratively referred to them as "boilers."

Chapter 9 Steamers and Boilers

The New York shore was indeed dotted with an increasing number of sails that propelled most of the vessels that navigated the waters of New York Bay. Then an inventor in Britain by the name of James Watt improved the steam engine, which could be used to power textile mills that eventually altered the textile and cotton industries. The steam train was an offshoot of Watt's steam engine. That extended the global distribution of populations and remapped and refaced the world to what we see it today.

It wasn't the first time that steam had been used to create mechanical motion of a repetitive nature. The original inventor of the steam engine had accomplished the feat a few decades earlier. Coincidently, it was the year that James Watt That steam engine was indeed the start of the Industrial Revolution—a revolution that shook the known world and caused a seismic shift in how civilizations were organized. It was the same revolution that brought mechanization to mills, factories, and transportation.

Once Watts had refined and improved the steam engine, it was adapted in many other ways. By 1783, the steam engine had been adapted to boats. It was first done by two Frenchmen new Lyon. By 1787, the idea of a boat powered by steam had made its way to New York, and the New York Legislature passed a law (Law of 1787) that gave the inventor of steamboats monopoly over steamboats in New York. John Fitch was awarded the monopoly for fourteen years to operate steamboats anywhere in New York. Ten years later, Robert Livingston licensed that monopoly and entered into a contract to build the steamboat in a foundry in New Jersey.

Livingston was the first man to put a steam vessel into the waters of New York Harbor and sail it up the Hudson to Albany. Livingston was sent to France as the ambassador for President Thomas Jefferson. In France, Livingstone met Robert Fulton, and the two of them entered into a contract in 1802 to build passenger steamboats to shuttle between Albany and New York by way of the Hudson River. The following year the first steamboat on the Seine River in France successfully navigated a portion of the river that runs through Paris. Then Fulton steamed to New York, and Livingston received an extension for this monopoly. In 1807, the *Clermont* steamed up the Hudson to Albany and returned to Manhattan in a total of four days. That successful trip prompted the New York Legislature to pass a law giving monopoly to Livingston and Fulton for a five-year period and an additional five years for each steam-propelled boat they deployed on the river, for a maximum of thirty years.

This monopoly was a stranglehold on the industry, as the state government also added a new law that impounded any steamship that was caught infringing on the monopoly during the time the case made its way through the courts. That grew extremely expensive for those who were tempted to infringe on the rights of Livingston and Fulton. It was 1811.

By 1817, Vanderbilt was being stretched thin and even considered retiring. Captain DeForest was no longer there to help him keep an eye on things. Managing all his vessels and the men in his employ was becoming difficult. The pilferage alone, by his workers, on the fleet that stretched from Albany inland to New England in the North and as far south as Savannah was becoming unmanageable. In all, historians calculate that he had saved up about $9,000 in cash and about $9,000 in assets. If he liquidated his position, he would hold $18,000, which is about $300,000 today. Vanderbilt was twenthy-three years old.

This event showcases another layer of Vanderbilt. He had worked himself so hard and acquired a sizeable sum, but he did not have anyone he could trust to manage it. He wasn't sure how to take the next step or what that step would even be. He had competition from the steamers that were becoming more common along the shore, and he was not able to keep tabs on his operations.

His first encounter with a steamer was when he intentionally purchased a ticket for a round-trip from Manhattan to Albany and back. He sat observing the new steamer and how it worked. It was obviously one of the Livingston-Fulton steamers. Even he had to agree that it was a much better ride than the periaugers he first started out with and even as good as one of his schooners.

His second encounter with a steamer was not under such congenial conditions. A Nor'easter—a strong storm that is endemic to New York and, in particular, the harbor area—had caught one of the steamers and sent her out of control heading down the Narrows. The steamer had also flooded, and the passengers were in grave danger. There weren't many boats in the water that day except for Vanderbilt who was sailing his schooner, *Dread.* A storm was not that important to him, but he saw that the steamer was in distress, and so he sailed up to her in the crosscurrents and windy bay and pulled off twelve shaken passengers and brought them to shore.

That event got his name in the papers the next morning as a hero. His fame spread even more than it already had. Then, a week later, his name appeared in the newspapers once again. This time the *Neptune* coming up from the southern coast carrying almost half a million dollars in currency and coin had run aground near Sandy Hook in a storm. The only boat that was in the area was the *Dread*, piloted once again by Vanderbilt. This time he went abeam the *Neptune*, boarded her, and rescued the crew and the boxes containing the cash. He then piloted the crew and money safely to shore.

Two rescues in one week in stormy conditions was unheard off and certainly something that attracted attention. One person who was interested was Thomas Gibbons.

Gibbons summoned Vanderbilt to his estate in Elizabeth, New Jersey, and Vanderbilt agreed. Gibbons was one of the wealthiest men in the country at the time, and Vanderbilt had heard of him. If he wanted to meet, one shouldn't decline.

When Vanderbilt met Gibbons, an instant bond formed in Vanderbilt's otherwise cold heart. Gibbons was all that Vanderbilt was except Gibbons was wealthy beyond what Vanderbilt had thought he himself could ever be. Meeting Gibbons at his estate redefined Vanderbilt's measure of wealth, and it cast a new light on the path that lay ahead for this young schooner pilot.

Until this point, Vanderbilt had been moving ahead on raw ambition, and his meeting with Gibbons now served to fine-tune his mind and give him direction. Gibbons offered him a job as captain of one of the steamers, the *Mouse*, for a tiny consideration. Most people would have declined, but Vanderbilt could see the future down this path, and so he took it. He would make just $60 a month.

He liquidated his schooners and sloops and all but one of the periaugers for an amount slightly less than what they were valued at. He got $7,000 (instead of $9,000) for them and went to work for Union Line.

Chapter 10 Steamboat Captain

Vanderbilt's decision to liquidate his proprietorship and take on employment may seem a setback in most eyes, but when you want to progress forward it is never an unrelenting march but rather a waltz that goes two steps forward, one step back, and then two forward again.

In the spirit of catching a breath and rubbing shoulders with one of the wealthiest men in the country, Vanderbilt's instinct to take this opportunity paid off, but he still had to put some muscle into it and work hard at what he was doing. This time Sophia helped.

Part of the deal between Gibbons and Vanderbilt was that he would move from Staten Island and live in a run-down tavern that he owned in Elizabeth, New Jersey. This establishment had been shuttered for some time and was in utter disrepair.

This was Sophia's new project. She was to polish it up and get it ready for business and then manage it. Gibbons would not charge them any rent but instead take 20 percent of the profits.

Vanderbilt had not paid attention to Sophia and left her on the sidelines to look after the Vanderbilt home and increase the famly's head count, but finally, she was in the game, and for some time she was actually doing better than Vanderbilt himself.

She managed to clean up the tavern, the kitchen, and the living quarters and then open it for business. She dealt with the cooking, the cleaning, and tended to the children all while she was pregnant in alternating years. In the third month since they moved in, Sophia had opened the doors to customers who were arriving by stagecoach in Elizabeth and waiting to take the ferry the next morning. The stagecoach was also one of Gibbons' operations, and the tavern was designed to be a waypoint where travelers could spend the night and get a warm meal. Within a month of opening the doors, Sophia was sending a pleasantly surprised Gibbons the 20 percent that was promised. The tavern did very well while Sophia looked after the business. She even kept the accounts and even better than Vanderbilt himself could keep with his vessels.

While she managed the tavern and took it from nothing to prosperity, Vanderbilt was out chasing his dreams. He was put to work on a tiny steamboat, an old ship that was much smaller than the other steamers in the harbor, but it was a start. Captain Vanderbilt had an opportunity to learn his way around sailing a larger boat. He had much to understand about balancing the hull and getting a feel for the steam output and speed that he could get from the boat.

The passengers soon started to complain, however, because of the dilapidated conditions of the boat. To compensate for that, Vanderbilt convinced Gibbons to reduce the fare, which he did, but that didn't last very long. Soon, the revenues started to drop, and Vanderbilt decided to put a case for a new boat to the owner.

He was successful, and Gibbons decided to commission a new steamer that displaced 140 tons, which was about five times the size of the old ship, and they decided to make something that was top of the line.

They sent the old boat in for repairs, and while the new boat and engine were being built, Vanderbilt had to monitor and make decisions on how the boat was to be designed. During this process, he made many alliances, from shipbuilders to steam engine fabricators, all of which would come in handy in the near future.

While the ship was being built, Vanderbilt still went back to his periauger and took on work for those who needed to ferry supplies around the bay. Between monitoring the construction of the new boat and sailing his tiny vessel, he was working sixteen to twenty hours a day, while Sophia managed the tavern and the children.

If nothing else, the Vanderbilts were a hardworking couple.

In due course, the new steamer was completed and put to water. The old steamer had also been repaired and refurbished, and now another captain was hired for it, and both ships sailed up and down the harbor. All was going well until the owners of the monopoly granted to Livingston and Fulton started to object.

A man by the name of Ogden decided to sue Gibbons for violating the monopoly granted by the State of New York to Livingston and then licensed to him. Gibbons knew what he was doing. Gibbons was a Federalist and a lawyer by training. He understood that the federal government had jurisdiction over this matter, and he was looking forward to filing his case in state court knowing that the judge would rule against him. He was right. The moment the court ruled he filed a petition with the New York Court of Errors (the older version of the state appeals court). Here, too, his case was found for the defendant but not without a little drama thrown in.

The states that were part of the union had only been so for the last forty years. Most of the arguments of states' rights versus federal rights were still being fought. Certain things were obviously states' rights, and the way the Constitution was worded was that all federal matters were explicitly stated therein. Anything that was not stated would be in the jurisdiction of the state.

The Court of Appeals judge, the plaintiff, and the defendant, as well as all the legal minds in New York who were following the case, including Gibbon's friend, the Attorney General of the United States, knew very well that the Supreme Court would decide to hear the case, and they also knew with fair certainty that the Supreme Court would rule in Gibbons' favor. For this reason, the Court of Appeals pulled off a delay strategy. They didn't rule on the case for three years. If there was no ruling, there would be no appeal.

In light of this underhanded tactic by Ogden and the court system, Gibbons, who also had a few friends in the New Jersey Legislature, got the state to enact legislation that would spite the New York crowd. He had already done this before when he got them to pass legislation that said that any law enforcement officer who incarcerated a New Jersey resident for piloting a boat would be arrested. It was intended to challenge the state of New York not to impound or incarcerate Gibbons' property or a person. This time they enacted legislation that would demand damages paid to New Jersey residents.

He also managed to get the New Jersey Legislature to disallow New York steamboats to ply the New Jersey shore and rivers. This effectively blocked the Livingston boats from navigating the waters down to Elizabeth and the other towns by the Raritan River

In the meantime, the shenanigans between New York steamship operators, the state legislators, and the mayor, who happened to be part of the Livingston clan, continued incessantly. They were all finding ways to stop Vanderbilt and impound Gibbons' steamship. Vanderbilt was smart enough never to let the boat that was in his charge be taken from him. If in the event he were captured, Gibbons would be present in short order to get him out of jail. This went on for the entire time Gibbons vs. Ogden remained undecided in the Court of Errors.

What's interesting about this is that Vanderbilt had played his cards well. He had framed the whole affair as a case of privilege over the working class. He framed it to appear that the entire state of New York was trying to place Vanderbilt under its heel. In time, Vanderbilt became a folk hero. His reputation was already solid in the bay area, but now he was a hero and a captain. He started to earn the name the Commodore.

In the end, the New York Court of Appeals ruled against Gibbons. At this point, he filed for an appeal in the U.S. Supreme Court. On his side was the Attorney General of the United States as well as a lawyer for Gibbons. They argued that Gibbons had the necessary licenses and permission to conduct business from New Jersey and into New York under the interstate commerce provision of the Constitution, and that he could not be barred by the state court.

Finally, after three years of delaying tactics by the Court of Errors, in 1823 the Supreme Court agreed with Gibbons, and the state's lower court judgment was overturned. Gibbons was able to keep sailing his steamships in and out of New York and New Jersey without any more obstruction.

Not only did Gibbons crack open the New York waterways but the decision handed down by the Supreme Court also shattered all the monopolies that Livingston had tied up in other waterways in the United States.

Chapter 11 Being One's Own Man

With the issue with the Supreme Court concluded and with Ogden out of business, Vanderbilt and Gibbons were free and clear to reap the benefits of an integrated line of transportation from Philadelphia to New York. Gibbons provided the carriages on land, and Vanderbilt navigated the rivers and the bay. Up in the morning and back in the afternoon.

The tavern Bellona Hall, which Sophia managed, was doing so well that she convinced Gibbons to invest another $3,000 to upgrade and extend the facilities. The tavern had been profitable ever since she took over, and Gibbons didn't hesitate for even a moment.

Vanderbilt's salary was raised to $300 per month from the initial $60. He still kept 20 percent of the bar's profits on all the steamboats, which at this point numbered three—the *Belona*, which was the 140-ton steamboat; the original smaller steamer that Vanderbilt initially stewarded, *Mouse*; and the latest and largest that was brought online, the *Thistle*. Two other captains had been employed to navigate the *Belona* and the *Mouse,* while Vanderbilt took on the significantly more luxurious and larger *Thistle*.

It was still a bargain for Gibbons, and there was a tacit understanding that when the time came Vanderbilt would be given a good deal on buying up the steamship business. There was nothing in writing and no handshake to seal the deal. In fact, it was one of Vanderbilt's only serious errors that he learned from and never committed again.

Just a few days before they took delivery of the largest steamship to sail between New York and New Brunswick—a behemoth of three levels and displacing two hundred tons—Gibbons passed away. In his last will and testament, he left the lion's share of his estate to his son. There was nothing in it for Vanderbilt, not even a severance package.

While Vanderbilt was not expecting anything, he did expect that when the time came William, Gibbons' son who inherited everything, including Union Line. Union Line was the company that employed Vanderbilt and owned the steamboats and Bellona Hall that Sophia managed.

The new steamboat they took delivery of was christened the *Emerald*. It came at a cost of $75,000. Vanderbilt took command of this behemoth and hired a new captain for the *Thistle*.

Before the *Emerald* came online, Union Line started attracting competitors for its New Brunswick/New York run. The new company had purchased Ogden's boats inexpensively but highly leveraged and hoped to beat Vanderbilt on the same route. There were distinct differences between the two companies. The first was that all but the *Emerald* were fully paid for. As for the new competitor, they had heavy interest and capital repayment schedules. As for speed, they were both equally matched. At first, Vanderbilt would take the morning line, and the competitor took the afternoon schedule, and there was not much conflict, but then they decided to go head-to-head in the schedule. In response, Vanderbilt sought and received permission to cut prices. He was back to his old tricks, and when all else failed, Vanderbilt always relied on price wars. It used to cost $5 to travel from Philadelphia to Manhattan. Vanderbilt dropped it to $2. For travel from New Brunswick to Manhattan, the trip used to cost seventy-five cents. He dropped it to thirteen cents.

At first, it seemed to work, but then the competitors dropped their price as well. Not to be outdone, Vanderbilt switched boats and put up the Bellona, which was fully paid for to compete and dropped the morning fare to zero. He also threw in free food.

After some resistance, the competitors were not sure what they could do since they couldn't go any lower on price, so they started to advertise faster trips. Vanderbilt continued to offer free trips and knew that his competitors were finding it hard to keep up. When they switched to competing on speed, Vanderbilt didn't bite. They started pressurizing their boilers artificially, meaning that they disabled the safety valve and made the steam build up to a higher point so that the paddles would be able to revolve faster. That was not a good idea, and the boilers exploded and killed a number of people on board.

Ticket sales dropped, as no one wanted to travel with them, and in just a few months they went out of business. Gibbons was impressed, and the rest of New York knew not to compete with the Commodore.

Vanderbilt and his wife put their heart and soul into the business, and they made money for everyone involved. Gibbons' son, who inherited everything, was not aware of any of this, as he was looking after the assets in his father's plantation in the South.

When Gibbons passed, the gratitude and relationship he had built with Vanderbilt did not translate to his son. William had no sense of camaraderie or admiration or even gratitude for that matter. It is not something the father would have discussed with his son.

Vanderbilt went on managing the business in the North, while William continued in the South. With everything going well, it came as a surprise when Vanderbilt heard in New York that Union Line had been put up for sale. William had not let Vanderbilt know beforehand.

To make matters worse, he had placed it on the open market and had set the price at $400,000 in cash. By this point, Vanderbilt only had 10 percent of that saved up.

What was working in his favor, though, was that everyone in the North knew that it was Vanderbilt who made that business work, and if he wasn't part of the deal, no one wanted to take the business off young William's hands. After keeping the sale alive for a few months, William took the Union Line off the market.

The precariousness of the situation was not lost on both Sophia and the Commodore. He had bought some time while he determined what to do, but William had shown his intentions. For whatever reason, he wanted to dispose of the business—most likely because he was not familiar with the operations or had too much going on in the South to bother with the smaller business in the North.

Whatever his reason, Vanderbilt had to prepare to set out on his own. It was at this point in his life that he swore to Sophia that he would never work for anyone else ever again. This time when he set out he would do it as his own man.

Chapter 12 What Goes Around

As wonderful a life as they had been living for ten years, Bellona Hall was not their home. It was the business that Sophia was managing and doing a good job, but that period was a critical stage in the lives of the Vanderbilt children, now numbering eight. They had made friends at school and had played in the river that was just behind the tavern. They had room to play, laugh, and grow up as children do.

Now they had to leave. It was the middle of December 1828. Vanderbilt was thirty-four years old and had decided to leave Union Line. He had saved $30,000 and by all measure was doing better than most men his age, but his miserly streak was becoming more prominent.

As soon as Vanderbilt had submitted his thirty days' notice to leave, William Gibbons went into a full-scale panic. He put all his steamboats up for sale at a fraction of the $400,000 he had so arrogantly priced the assets just a few months before. Vanderbilt arranged for the financing and bought two of the vessels—the *Bellona* and the *Emerald*. He was also able to raise enough financing to commission a new steamboat, which was one of the largest at that time. It was displacing 240 tons and was luxurious and well outfitted. It was personally designed by Vanderbilt, and he made it in such a way that the hull was designed to slice through the water in the front. It was hydrodynamically sound and one of the fastest in its class.

When they moved to Manhattan, they moved to a part of town that was more like the slums than it was the well-heeled side of New York. Vanderbilt's actions here should be heeded by any entrepreneur. Even though he had what was equivalent to three quarters of a million dollars in today's money, when he left Bellona Hall, he was not willing to spend $300 a year on rental, which would have put his family in a nice neighborhood, one suitable for the children and a family environment. Instead, they took a three-bedroom apartment in a building that was tenanted by dock workers and laborers with as many as twenty people to an apartment. Conditions were horrible, but Sophia, who was still reeling from losing the one thing that had brought her joy and accomplishment, made do. There is no indication that she had any idea that her husband had that much money saved. She had some savings as well from the money she had been making at the tavern.

Vanderbilt chose that location for two important reasons: (1) his ships were docked nearby on the Hudson and (2) and more important was that he was stepping into the unknown. He obviously had plans, but there was no sense in spending money when it could be used to expand and develop a business. The problem was that he still didn't have a good fix on what the business would be.

He knew it would involve steamboats, but he also had to think about other things. He needed to consider the route and the operations, and with all that still in the air, it was better to be frugal than to live it up in the city and not have any idea of what the future would hold.

It took him less than a few months to get things in order, and this is when he bought the four ships. He had decided to sail the same route he had been while under the employ of Gibbons. He was familiar with the landscape as well as the businesses that lined the river and the clientele that he would engage. The problem was that he didn't buy all of the Union Line boats. He only bought two. The others were sold to a businessman from Philadelphia who had known the Gibbons family well. He took on the rest of the boats and became a direct competitor to Vanderbilt.

As before, a price war erupted. This time Vanderbilt was outmatched and outfinanced. In a classic case of karma, what goes around had come back around, but Vanderbilt didn't believe in karma. He believed in winning. Vanderbilt was facing the same issues with price cutting, but he had a different plan and a different strategy. He continued to cut his price. In the last instance, the strategy was to beggar the competition, but this time it was different. He knew the competitor well enough to instinctively know that if given enough trouble that person would buy him out. In one year, that is exactly what happened. He bought two of Vanderbilt's boats for cash and royalties made from the New Brunswick/Manhattan line.

It was the first time that someone had literally paid Vanderbilt to stop working, and it wouldn't be the last.

He took the money he made from the sale of these two boats and bought two more. He was back to four boats, but this time he decided it was time to take on a new route. He decided to go up the Hudson, but he faced another hurdle.

The Supreme Court had ruled in Ogden vs. Gibbons that federal law trumps state law in interstate commerce—the steamboats that traveled between New Jersey and New York. The Constitution could not regulate commerce within the state, however, which meant that the unholy alliance of Livingston and Fulton that caused the monopoly to be in place was unaffected by the Supreme Court ruling.

Supreme Court ruling notwithstanding, the monopoly that was created by the New York Legislature was not popular, and it hinted of unfavorable practice by one of New York's wealthy and influential families. By 1827, the winds of change had swept the Livingston-Fulton monopoly to the rocks, and the waterways were once again back to competitive forces.

It was at this point that Vanderbilt took his four ships and set them to travel on the Hudson from Albany to Manhattan. He now faced a new competitor, and he fought back.

He named his venture "The People's Line" to sway public sentiment against this monopoly that was operated by some powerful and wealthy backers. The plan worked. Vanderbilt was able to stir the hornet's nest of class warfare.

He won again and continued expanding his line, commissioning more steamboats to travel between Albany and Manhattan. The Erie Canal had been completed, and the effect increased the growth rate of New York and the transportation business between the two cities.

It was all going well when he had to go to Philadelphia on business. He decided to take the train to see what all the excitement was about with this new mode of transportation. It is rumored that he shared the trip with President Quincy Adams, who was in the coach just ahead of him.

The train was speeding along its tracks at almost twenty-five miles per hour. Compared to a stagecoach, it was floating on a cushion of air, and there was plenty of room to sit comfortably. As the train approached a ravine and began its transition to a wooden bridge, something serious happened.

The iron tracks on the unstable wooden platform started to come loose after the heavy locomotive and the first car had passed. The second and third car were not so fortunate. The couplings came loose as the second car came off the tracks and plunged down a thirty-foot ravine. Most people in the second and third cars died. Vanderbilt was not one of them, but he did break a few ribs and was severely injured.

He was transported back to New York, where he spent his time recuperating for the better part of the following year. It was too much for Sophia to handle on her own, so she had her cousin live with them in their small apartment to help with the chores while she nursed the Commodore back to health.

A doctor was chosen for him, a young man who would eventually become one of Vanderbilt's closest friends. The doctor would visit almost daily at first to tend to the wounds and monitor his progress. As Vanderbilt regained his strength, the doctor visited less often.

He had hired another captain to take his place as captain on the *Bellona*, and he continued to run the other vessels as well. He was now thinking of expanding his route eastward into Long Island Sound to be able to move up to Connecticut and possibly even Boston, which was also a busy harbor, and the route that hugged the New England coast was fairly lucrative.

Just before the accident, he had bought the southern routes between Elizabeth, New Brunswick, and Philadelphia. Those routes added to the opportunistic trading he did for cargo on short hauls and products from the fishermen along the shore and helped his business thrive. His reputation also allowed him to have a ready line of credit, which was useful anytime he wanted to buy a used steamboat or commission a new one.

Each time he entered a new market the same formula applied. He or the current dominant service in that market would initiate a price war. It had become Vanderbilt's legacy to wage these wars, and he hardly ever lost one.

He had understood early on that the key to long-term gain was to have a dominant market share as quickly as possible. Regardless of the cost on the front end, which could translate as a loss for some period of time, the end result was worth the initial hardship.

He had learned with Gibbons' boats the value of fully paid assets and the way to trounce any competitor who was highly leveraged. It turns out that most of the boat owners at the time had financed their boats and were under the heel of interest payments.

That was partially the reason why he was always very frugal with how he spent money. His cash reserves were actually worth more than the value of the cash. It was worth the making or breaking of the route that he ventured on. In case of competition, the person who could outlast a war would be the one to reap the benefits. The person who could last the longest was the person who had the least financial obligations and depended on the cash flow from the business to sustain.

For most people, it was one of two things. It was either a bank loan they had to sustain or a family they had to support. It was also that many of the boat owners focused too much on one particular route.

Focusing on just a single route placed one's entire asset base in competition with the other person, and it was like a duel at noon. One person either lost everything or gained everything. In those days, losing everything was not a good option, especially in New York, where there were such things as debtors prisons. Ogden had faced a similar fate when he went up against Gibbons and lost. He had invested heavily and then borrowed more to compete and fight the lengthy court battle, and when he lost to Gibbons, in the end, he had no way of paying off his debtors and went to prison for it.

Vanderbilt was acutely aware of all this. Aside from the fear of taking on a loan he couldn't pay, he was aware of the loss that he would face in the event of stiff competition. He was setting himself up to lose the entire business if he borrowed too much or got used to spending too much. Vanderbilt knew that cash was king.

For his strategy, the more reserves he had, the less he borrowed, and the leaner his operations were, the longer he could wage a war that may have included free travel and free food for as long as he needed to drive away the competitor.

The trick was to also spread his ships around different markets. He had already conquered the Philadelphia/Delaware market. He had definitely conquered the New Brunswick/Manhattan market, and he was already set up to conquer the Hudson/Albany market, and now it was up to New England.

By the time he had spread his proverbial sail to the four corners of the Northeast, other operators had learned from him and were vicious in their war on price. What went around had come around. He had to deal with the same strategies that he had grown to adopt.

The difference between Vanderbilt and every other single steamship operator was that Vanderbilt had one thing going for him—his mind-set. He never cared about living the good life. He only cared to save his money. This gave him little reliance on how much he had to make from the fare. He would just as easily make the fare zero, while his other competitors could not. To do this, he had learned to become one of the best cash managers in the business.

Chapter 13 The Advent of Rail

The advent of rail in America was the driving force behind the development of the interior of the country. Before this time, there were two population dispersion patterns. The first reflected people living along coastlines. With a series of canals, such as the Erie canal that connects Manhattan to Albany and proceeds on to the Great Lakes, it allowed more people to move inland, but vast areas were still unpopulated. There were occasional outposts and frontier settlements, but those areas would remain sparsely settled until the arrival of the train. As railway lines started to make tracks inland, the population also increased.

The same could be said for the major rivers and waterways all along the eastern portion of the United States. Vanderbilt had a front-row seat to the development of the rail industry in the United States. Instead of being the death of steamships, railroads actually enhanced the industry. Rails could not reach certain parts of the country, and other areas were inaccessible for steamships. Both had their strengths and weaknesses, and this complementary relationship increased the freedom of travel and access for the masses.

The much older Vanderbilt now planned his boats around the trains and stagecoaches. When the Boston-Providence Railroad went into service, Vanderbilt had commissioned new boats that were larger, more luxurious, and faster to travel the two hundred miles from New York to Providence. This allowed him to provide almost seamless travel from Philadelphia all the way to Boston under a single fare. Passengers would travel from Philadelphia to New Brunswick and then from there to Manhattan. From Manhattan, they would board the new steamer that would travel at top speeds of twenty miles per hour up to Indian Point in Providence. Then they would board the train that went straight to Boston. Vanderbilt had brought the far-flung cities just a little closer. In the center of it all was New York—his stomping ground.

New York's growth in the 1800s was spurred by three factors, one of which was Vanderbilt's doing.

(1) New York served as the port of influx of immigrants and products and also the point for export of all raw materials and finished goods.

(2) The Erie Canal allowed travel up to the Great Lakes and then down again to western Pennsylvania. In the days before rail travel, this was the least treacherous route even if it did take more than a week to make the journey.

(3) Vanderbilt's organization of steamboats and their coinciding schedules to meet with stagecoaches was also important. The comparative ease of travel from one major town to the next, with stops in all the smaller towns, altered the way people conducted business and forced the different states to come together as one nation.

It was not any form of altruism that caused Vanderbilt to take on these routes or to have this kind of impact. He didn't wake up one morning and have the epiphany that he wanted to build in a nation instead of a fragmented set of states. He didn't have the nationalistic streak in him to do that, and he also didn't have the academic background to consider that. He saw the world as one big series of transactions, and he just wanted to do what was best for him.

Central to his plan of making the trips almost seamless was his ability to have no problems at Indian Point in Providence. The station and the wharf were right next to each other, and the transition was as good as could be. People would disembark at the wharf and then take a short walk to the platform to catch their train. It was perfect except for one small glitch. Once again the powers that be, in this case the Providence legislative circles, were not interested in having Vanderbilt frequent their town and compete with the business their group and cabals had planned. They caused him as much trouble as they could. Vanderbilt did not care much about what they were doing, though, and he would do what he had to as he had when Livingstone and New York were giving him and Gibbons trouble.

In Providence, he just started doing what he wanted to do.

At the same time, another rag-to-riches kind of person by the name of Grinnell had set up another ferry service that stretched from Boston to Providence. There was some traffic that frequented the Grennel steamboat, but it wasn't as profitable as it could be. Most travelers preferred the train for the same price. Besides, Grennell's boat just went to Providence and didn't go on to New York. They would still have to change carriers.

With all the trouble that Providence was giving Vanderbilt, he decided to try something new. Instead of engaging in a price war—there was no one to wage war with because his competitors were not the ones causing the problem—he came up with a new scheme. Instead of predatory pricing, he engaged in collusion.

He approached Grennell and made a deal with him to charge customers the same price from Boston to New York, but instead of stopping at Providence, he would stop at Stonington. Vanderbilt would then sail up to Stonington, and the passengers would transfer from one boat to another and go all the way down to New York. Together, they would charge a dollar less than the train/ferry combination that customers would have to take.

The plan was a success, and passengers were more than happy to pay a dollar less for the same trip. This plan pulled customers away from the Boston/Providence rail line, and it also precipitously reduced the number of passengers that came into Providence. That had a more serious impact. With lower passenger traffic in Providence, the city was worried that it would attract less revenue for the city.

Vanderbilt had learned a long time before that the value of a line was not just in the price of the ticket that a person paid. In fact, it was even acceptable to accept a loss for the price of the ticket because the bar and café on board, especially on a twelve-hour trip, made substantial revenue to cover part of the cost of the pinewood needed to fire the boilers.

This was the same logic that the Providence town managers had in mind. The revenue they generated from the mere traffic of passengers arriving and spending money at the wharf was considered good income for the city. With Vanderbilt's new plan, Providence would be affected by fewer passenger arrivals, but it didn't matter that Vanderbilt's passenger traffic was at an all-time high.

A few years later he sold the steamship that would make the New York-Stonington run to Grennel himself, and he replaced it with a 500-ton steamer. That same year after the sale the ship burst into flames while anchored in Long Island Sound. Out of the two hundred passengers and crew on board, only four survived.

Even though he had redirected his business to circumvent the rail, Vanderbilt still fully realized the power of the railroad and the even greater power of the combination of the railroad and steamship. For now, however, he focused on steamboats.

By 1840, his wealth had grown. He now made more almost $40,000 a year in profit and was worth almost $1.5 million, which would be about

$40 million today. While the lion's share of his wealth came from the income from the steamships, he had also invested in land up and down the New Jersey coast as well as in Manhattan. From the people who boarded his steamships to the children playing in the wharf, everyone knew him as the Commodore. He was only forty-six years old and more successful than any of the Vanderbilts before him.

Nothing controlled him, and nothing could compete against him. As the years passed, the only thing that would dictate the routes he took were the railroads and the timing of the trains. He didn't need them, but when he worked in concert with them, he realized that the passenger traffic was high, and that appealed to him. In his mind, it didn't matter if he was not making any money right then. It was more important to fill his ships. Capacity utilization, as any MBA student will tell you, is the key to long-term profitability and value even when the short term looked bleak. Those who tried to mimic him did not always succeed. Vanderbilt knew how to keep his vessels full and make money in the long term. He knew when to hold and when to let go, and when the time came to let go, he did it without any hesitation or remorse.

By 1845, the Long Island Railroad had been completed all the way from Brooklyn to the farthest tip in the east—at Greenpoint. The point of the railroad was not to serve any of the Long Island towns. There weren't as many when the line was first built as there are today. Once the line was built, it was mainly meant for traffic to go all the way to the farthest reach of the island and then transfer the passengers to a steamship so that they could then sail up to Boston. At this point, Vanderbilt's fortunes changed He was invited to sit on the board of directors of the Long Island Railroad (LIRR).

This move was beneficial for the LIRR and for Vanderbilt. For the LIRR, it meant they would have a steady passenger load from Brooklyn to Greenpoint, where they would then be transferred to the Commodore's steamboats and sent northbound. That was the plan, but it got better. Instead, Vanderbilt sold two of his steamers to the LIRR. They used these to carry passengers from the edge of Long Island up to Norwich, where they would then board the Boston Norwich line and head straight to Boston.

Thereafter at Vanderbilt's behest, the LIRR partnered with the owners of the Boston Norwich line and offered a packaged deal that would go from Brooklyn all the way to Boston for just $4. All they had to do was get to Greenpoint, take the short ferry ride across Long Island Sound, and then board the train in Norwich. From there it was a straight shot to Boston. No one could compete with that, and it became the preferred route for all Boston-New York passengers. His interest had begun to shift from steamships to the railroad. It wouldn't be long before he would immerse himself in the railroad industry, and he would do it by way of something called the stock market.

Chapter 14 Better Quarters

Ever since the day when the entire family of ten—eight children and two adults—left the comfort and safety of Bellona Hall, Sophia had been gently, albeit persistently, lobbying for better quarters. The home they lived in on Madison Avenue (as hard as it is to believe now) was a putrid place. It didn't just look run-down. It was one of the worst tenements on the island. It housed some of the hardest roughnecks the city had come to accommodate, and it was packed well beyond what it was designed to hold. The stench of the facilities on one floor would stretch across several floors and spread like a green mist. It was not what the Vanderbilt children who had grown up amidst the clean air of the river and densely wooded forest of Elizabeth, New Jersey, could get used to.

But Vanderbilt was on a mission. It was more important to him that they had a home than to live on the street, which is what they would end up doing if they were not careful with their resources and didn't use what they had to invest in future businesses. Besides, Sophia really had no idea how much he had saved.

Finally, in 1839, just before becoming a director of the LIRR, she had whittled away any form of resistance that he had been putting up. He was also motivated because he was doing better, and his business, while competitive, had sucked the energy out of him, and he felt better about his future prospects.

They moved back to Staten Island, where he built a mansion of such palatial proportions that Sophia could not fathom how he did it, and it was the first time she began to understand just how wealthy they had become. He commissioned the construction of a mansion on the shore at the northeastern corner of Staten Island near the same spot that his mother and father had first bought their home when they moved to the island so long before. The house was magnificently designed, no doubt fueled by the imagination that sparked from his visit to Gibbons' estate when he was still skimming the harbor in his schooners and periauger. The house was built at cost of just under $30,000 and had ornate furnishings, stained glass windows, tall Greek columns to support the large roof, Egyptian marble in the floors and mantle, grand staircases that were intricately designed by masons with banisters carved by expensive craftsmen, French drapes hanging from vaulted ceilings, and a skylight in the ceiling to illuminate the cavernous home. There were four floors and a basement, each with twelve-foot ceilings that welcomed light from the skylight and breeze from the tall open windows that overlooked the Narrows on one side and the bay on the other. It was the view he had admired when he was three years old, looking at the colorful sails that went past his window every day. The view had changed. Now it was rows of steamers puffing smoke from burning coal and steam rising from boilers.

The house was the monolithic depiction of this simple man—the Commodore. It was visibly strong, tall, and substantial. Visitors were in awe, but Sophia wasn't. Little did she know that she would eventually die in this house all alone.

Sophia didn't say anything about the house, and Vanderbilt really didn'tcare one way or the other. She had other things on her mind. Her health had not been in the best condition for some time, and she was exhausted. Between the dilapidated conditions of the tenement, giving birth to a large number of children, nursing, and then looking after them while Vanderbilt himself was out building his business and spending some of his time in the company of transactional women, she was getting sicker by the day.

She was diagnosed with syphilis in 1840. She was already aware that her husband was cavorting with a wide array of women on the wharf, but she didn't realize that it would come to this. It was not just her physical state that was deteriorating but also her mental state. Between her menopausal years that would come quickly and the complications from syphilis, she had become an altogether different woman.

In reaction to her deterioration, Vanderbilt first threatened and then carried out the act of committing her to an asylum. Both business and family carried on for the next decade with more of the same. Billy had grown up and had disappointed his father. It took a lot to satisfy Vanderbilt with anything his children did, but that is not to be misunderstood. As a man who had made his own way from the time he was eleven years old, he was always hard on his children so that they would be able to show a fraction of his tenacity in making their own way. He may have been stingy to an extent, but that doesn't seem to be the reason why he cut off most of his children. It was more because he was of the frame of mind that that was the best way to teach them how to survive in a tough world. Vanderbilt himself, if he had to be described with one word, would bring to mind "tough." He indeed was tough not just in fistfights but in the mental sense of the word as well. Nothing was able to knock him off his saddle, but if by chance something did, he was back up on it again in short order.

One example of this is when one of his children who behaved in a way that was slow Vanderbilt would not stand for it. He got the boy a job at a Wall Street firm, and as a favor to Vanderbilt, the firm employed him at a small salary that was fully subsidized by Vanderbilt. He did it to get the boy to feel confident of his own ability. That confidence, however, was misplaced, as his son thought he should be able to get married. He found a wife and decided to marry her without his father's approval. He had no idea that his salary was being subsidized by Vanderbilt himself.

Once they were married, Vanderbilt decided his son could not live on a small salary with a wife, and so he bought the farmland that was near his grandfather's in New Dorp. It was almost eighty-nine acres. Vanderbilt presented it to his son and daughter-in-law and told him to never ask for money again. He was to work the land and support his wife and family. The two never spoke after that.

The point is that it is not easy to get into the heart of a man and understand what drives him to do certain things. He may not have seemed to love his family, but it is not for us to say that he did or didn't. We also do not know if he was really capable of loving.

What we do know, though, is that despite his proclivities he was a man who worked hard and provided for his family. For those who say that he left Sophia to raise the children, you have to balance that by considering he was building a business and working 16-hour days. Not many people can work that number of hours in the cold and rain on many days, wet from the waters of the bay, and then come home and have the strength to display magnanimity or patience.

Conclusion

Prospectors found gold in the Sierra Nevada Mountains in 1849. This resulted in the Gold Rush that year, as entire families with gold in their eyes rushed to the West Coast to find their fortune. The trek west was hard. There weren't many waterways and only a few outposts along the way that served the crowds that made their way across dense forests, hot deserts, and some of the most picturesque mountains in North America.

Vanderbilt saw it another way. He didn't see gold as the holy grail. He saw the money he could make by transporting people who were going after the gold. His logic was simple. By providing those prospectors with a service, he was assured of his payment. By digging for the gold himself, it was a long shot. So he decided to be the man who would transport the prospectors heading west. There was one problem: no waterway was available.

Instead, he looked at how the U.S. government was having mail transported to the West Coast. They were doing it by sea. Since the way to the West Coast by sea would take the ship all the way down to Cape Horn in South America and then back up, it was considered too long to make the trip. It would take about six months to a year for a ship of fifty people to make it.

The mail ships had a better way of doing it. They would sail down to the slimmest part of the isthmus in Panama, and then passengers would go overland until they reached the Pacific shore. Then they would take another boat up to California. The overland phase of the trip would be through forests, and they managed it with a train of mules. It was only fifty miles, and they could do it in about a week.

This idea appealed to the pragmatic Commodore. Instead of using the Panama route, however, he went to Nicaragua and negotiated a twelve-year contract with them where he would build a canal in the 80-mile crossing from east to west, and then he would own the rights to that passageway. The deal was struck. He would pay

Nicaragua $10,000 in cash and $10,000 every year and $20,000 in company stock. It would take twelve years to build the canal. Once built, Nicaragua would then take 20 percent of the profits, and the rights would extend for eighty-five years. Vanderbilt also included a clause that stipulated that in the event the canal could not be built he would be able to build some other route of transportation, such as a railway track to cross the isthmus.

In 1850, he set sail from New York to Nicaragua for a test run. The plan was to reach the west coast of Nicaragua and then sail up the San Juan River to Lake Nicaragua, which was close to the western coast. When they reached the river, Vanderbilt himself navigated the vessel at full speed with the boiler valve locked in place. No boilers blew on that trip. Instead, all the power was transported to the paddles, and the vessel made record time over the rapids and to the lake 199 miles inland. Vanderbilt was the first man to take a steamship up the San Juan River. On board with him were the engineers who were to study the route and decide where to blast and make the river deeper or smoothen the rapids.

When they returned to New York, he was deemed a hero. From here on, he would charge customers who wanted to sail to San Francisco from New York for $399 compared with $600 charged by those who were using Panama. He also made it to California faster than they did. He had brought his New York price war to Central America. The price eventually dropped to $145 for deck customers and $45 for steerage.

In time, he saw that it was more profitable even in the midst of an all-out price war to focus on the Nicaragua passage, which he called the Southern Route. He slowly and quietly started divesting his other New York ships. He still maintained his railroad interests and investments.

What started in the 1840s as a side interest was now gaining traction for Vanderbilt. While the southern route continued and prospered, he started working on the railroads in New York. He began buying railroad stocks and organized them to make it more efficient, and to do that he designed and built Grand Central Station.

In the end, he was confined to the upstairs bedroom in his midtown townhouse. It was the fall of 1876, and syphilis had caught up with him. He was in end-stage syphilis just like Sophia, who had died in 1868. By Christmas, he was bedridden and sometimes incoherent. He died January 7, 1877. At all schools, government offices, and buildings—anywhere where a flag flew—the flag was flown at half-staff.

Made in the USA
Middletown, DE
12 November 2019